# RACHEL ZEGLER

BY MARY BLECKWEHL

AMICUS LEARNING

**Inspire is published by**
**Amicus Learning, an imprint of Amicus**
P.O. Box 227
Mankato, MN 56002
www.amicuspublishing.us



**Editor:** Ana Brauer
**Series Designer:** Kathleen Petelinsek
**Book Designer and Photo Researcher:** Emily Dietz

**Library of Congress Cataloging-in-Publication Data**
Names: Bleckwehl, Mary E. author
Title: Rachel Zegler / by Mary Bleckwehl.
Description: Mankato, MN : Amicus Learning, an imprint of Amicus, 2026. | Series: Inspire | Includes bibliographical references and index. | Audience: Ages 5–9 | Audience: Grades 2–3 | Summary: "From high school musicals to Hollywood stardom! Discover how Rachel Zegler became a breakout star in *West Side Story*, *The Hunger Games: The Ballad of Songbirds and Snakes*, and *Snow White*. Includes table of contents, glossary, further resources, and index"— Provided by publisher.
Identifiers: LCCN 2025011918 (print) | LCCN 2025011919 (ebook) | ISBN 9798892008648 library binding | ISBN 9798892009300 paperback | ISBN 9798892009966 ebook
Subjects: LCSH: Zegler, Rachel, 2001—Juvenile literature | Motion picture actors and actresses—United States—Biography—Juvenile literature | Singers—United States—Biography—Juvenile literature | LCGFT: Biographies
Classification: LCC PN2287.Z44 B54 2026 (print) | LCC PN2287.Z44 (ebook) | DDC 791.4302/8092 [B]—dc23/eng/20250527
LC record available at https://lccn.loc.gov/2025011918
LC ebook record available at https://lccn.loc.gov/2025011919

**Photo Credits:** Alamy Stock Photo/Album, 8, Collection Christophel, 14, Media Punch, cover, Photo12/7e Art/Warner Bros Television, 5; Getty Images/Arnold Jerocki, 7, Gotham, 17, John Nacion/Variety, 19, JULIEN DE ROSA, 16, Mike Marsland, 10, Murray Close, 13, River Callaway, 9, XNY/Star Max, 4, 20; Playbill Inc/unknown , 21



**Printed in the United States of America**

# Table of Contents

5 Starstruck
6 Singing Her Way Through School
9 Giant Leap to Stardom
11 Shazam!
12 A Rising Star
15 A New Snow White
16 Facing the Music
18 A Voice of Change
21 A Shiny Future
22 Super Stats
23 Glossary
24 Read More
24 On the Web
24 Index

**Rachel Zegler is famous for her roles in musicals, including *West Side Story*.**

# Starstruck

A four-year-old girl sat on the edge of her seat. It was her first time at a Broadway show. Her eyes were glued to the actors. Belle looked like a real princess. The Beast was BIG. The girl loved it. She grew up and still loves theater. She is Rachel Zegler, an American actress and singer.

**DID YOU KNOW?**
**Zegler was named after Rachel Green, a character on the TV show *Friends*.**

# Singing Her Way Through School

Zegler loved to sing and knew she wanted to be an actress. Her talent landed her roles in high school musicals. She played Belle in *Beauty and the Beast* and Ariel in *The Little Mermaid*. She even sang at weddings and funerals. Her goal was to sing on Broadway.

**SOCIAL MEDIA STAR**

**Zegler posted song covers on YouTube. Her cover of "Shallow" by Lady Gaga and Bradley Cooper received over 12 million views on Twitter.**

Zegler began acting in plays at a young age, showcasing her talent early on.

Zegler and Ansel Elgort starred in the 2021 remake of *West Side Story*.

# Giant Leap to Stardom

A friend of Zegler's told her a movie was holding **auditions**. It was for the role of Maria in *West Side Story* (2021). Zegler decided to try. She sent in a recording of herself. 30,000 people tried out, but she got the part! She was just 17.

**DID YOU KNOW?**
At 20 years old, Zegler was the youngest person to win a **Golden Globe** for Best Actress in a Motion Picture – Musical or Comedy.

Unlike her singing roles in other projects, Zegler doesn't sing in ***Shazam! Fury of the Gods*** **(2023).**

# Shazam!

After her movie **debut**, Zegler was getting noticed. But a **pandemic** hit. She auditioned from home over **Zoom** for a part. She was picked to be in *Shazam! Fury of the Gods* (2023). Her role was the goddess, Anthea.

# A Rising Star

More parts came Zegler's way. In 2023, she starred in *The Hunger Games: The Ballad of Songbirds and Snakes*. As Lucy Gray Baird, she played a singer who became a brave fighter.

In 2023, Zegler took on a leading role in *The Hunger Games* **prequel**.

Zegler played Snow White in the live-action remake of Disney's 1937 movie.

# A New Snow White

Zegler sang her way into a Disney classic. She played Snow White in the 2025 live-action movie. Viewers saw changes from the original. Zegler's skin wasn't white. Snow White didn't get saved by a prince. Some liked the changes. Others didn't.

# Facing the Music

People listen to actors. Zegler spoke up about the Snow White movie and her role. She feels it shows that girls don't need to be saved. They can be leaders.

**DID YOU KNOW?**
Zegler is a **Swiftie**! Both singers use their voices to make a difference.

Zegler supports SAG-AFTRA, an actor's union. She joined others during a 2023 strike to fight for fair pay.

Zegler speaks out on social issues and encourages others to make a positive difference.

# A Voice of Change

Zegler is a Latina actress. She's happy kids can see someone who looks like them on screen. She wants her roles and words to be meaningful. She's proud her face and voice can bring change.

**DID YOU KNOW?**
Zegler was the first Latina actress to play Maria in *West Side Story*.

In 2025, Zegler starred in the musical *Evita* on London's West End.

# A Shiny Future

Rachel Zegler did make it to Broadway. In 2024, she played Juliet in *Romeo + Juliet*. Zegler has shown she can act and sing almost anything. Her brave and bubbly voice has only begun to shine. Let's see where it leads.

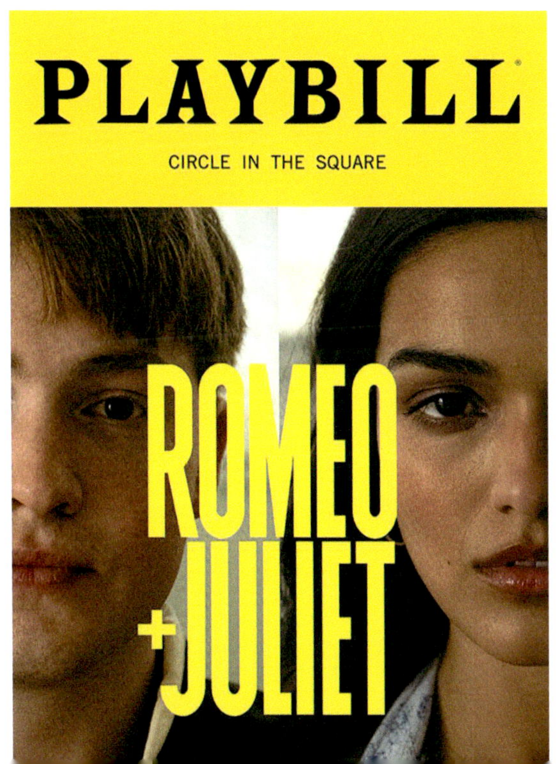

# SUPER STATS

## RACHEL ANNE ZEGLER

**Birthday:** May 3, 2001

**Birthplace:** Hackensack, NJ

**Home:** New York City, NY

**Major Film Roles:** *West Side Story* (2021), *The Hunger Games: The Ballad of Songbirds & Snakes* (2023), *Shazam: Fury of the Gods* (2023), *Spellbound* (2024), *Snow White* (2025)

**Professional Theater:** *Romeo + Juliet* (2024), *Evita* (2025)

## MAJOR AWARDS

**Golden Globe:** 2022

**People's Choice Award:** 2024

**iHeartRadio Music Award:** 2025

# GLOSSARY

**audition** A tryout for a performing part.

**cover** A new recording of a song by someone other than the original performer.

**debut** A person's first time performing.

**pandemic** Time of widespread infectious disease.

**prequel** An installment in a series of books or movies which describes action that occurred in the past, before the original.

**Swiftie** A fan of singer-songwriter Taylor Swift.

**Zoom** A video conferencing platform on the internet.

# READ MORE

Bisantz, Max. **What Is the Story of Romeo and Juliet?** Penguin Workshop, 2023.

Jimenez, Bruce L. **RACHEL ZEGLER: Shining Bright on Stage and Screen,** 2024.

# ON THE WEB

**Kiddle: Rachel Zegler**
https://kids.kiddle.co/Rachel_Zegler

**Official YouTube Channel**
https://www.youtube.com/@RachelZeglerLovesHugs

Every effort has been made to ensure that these websites are appropriate for children. However, because of the nature of the Internet, it is impossible to guarantee that these sites will remain active indefinitely or that their contents will not be altered.

# INDEX

auditions, 9, 11
*Ballad of Songbirds and Snakes*, 12–13
Broadway, 5, 6, 21
Golden Globes, 9
high school, 6
Latina, 18
movies, 9, 11, 14, 15, 16
musicals, 4, 6, 9, 20
*Shazam! Fury of the Gods*, 10–11
*Snow White*, 14–15, 16
*West Side Story*, 4, 8–9, 18

## About the Author

Mary Bleckwehl is a children's author who loves cookie dough and talking to kids. She is happiest when she is biking and exploring new places. Mary lives in Minnesota with her husband and monster dog. Check out her books at marybleckwehl.com.